A former president of Oxford Un
cal Society, Jack Jones read history
university before going on to work i
ter and at Carisbrooke Castle. Now i
near Newport and he keeps his intere.   . uadcasting
(as a *Round Britain Quiz* panellist) and in writing. He is
the author of *The Royal Prisoner: Charles I at Carisbrooke* and, jointly with his wife Johanna, *The Isle of
Wight: An Illustrated History*, which was also published
by the Dovecote Press.

Isle of Wight Curiosities

Jack Jones

THE DOVECOTE PRESS

First published in 1989 by The Dovecote Press Ltd
Stanbridge, Wimborne, Dorset BH21 4JD
ISBN 0 946159 67 X

Photoset in Times by Character Graphics, Taunton, Somerset
Printed and bound by Biddles Ltd, Guildford and King's Lynn

Contents

Introduction

'Desire to know why, and how, curiosity, which is a lust of the mind, that by a perseverance of delight in the continued and indefatigable generation of knowledge, exceedeth the short vehemence of any carnal pleasure.'

All that Thomas Hobbes was saying in his *Leviathan* was that humankind is made with a printed circuit of inquisitiveness; and an unfailing focus of curiosity is *a* curiosity, something that does not quite fit the usual pattern. We want to know why, and how.

This quality of curiosities, the capacity to make our minds buzz, overrides their other qualities. They can be important or trivial, significant or merely quaint. This means that there is scope for variety, and the Isle of Wight has always had plenty of that. Its extraordinary surface geology is reflected in a great range of scenery and habitat, a variety of flora and fauna, and the Islanders seem to have taken their cue from this in the way local society has developed, often unpredictably. 'The isle is full of noises, sounds and sweet airs, that give delight, and hurt not.' Shakespeare's Caliban might have been talking about the Isle of Wight.

Here is a selection, then, of some of the local quaintnesses that have give me pleasure and interest, and I hope you will enjoy sharing them – if they are not familiar to you already. Inevitably I have relied very much on advice from those who know the Island much better than I do, and I would specially like to thank Roy Brinton, Oliver Frazer, Patrick Nott, Kitty Page, Bill Shepard, Clifford Webster, Graham Wynne of British Telecom, and – not least – my wife Johanna for her continual help and advice. Any mistakes that have eluded this screening are blameable on me.

Grateful acknowledgement is made to the following for permissions for and help with the illustrations:

The Vicar of Carisbrooke (21)
The Vicar of Newport (17, 23, 55)
The Priest in charge of Shorwell (40)
The Vicar of Yarmouth (10)

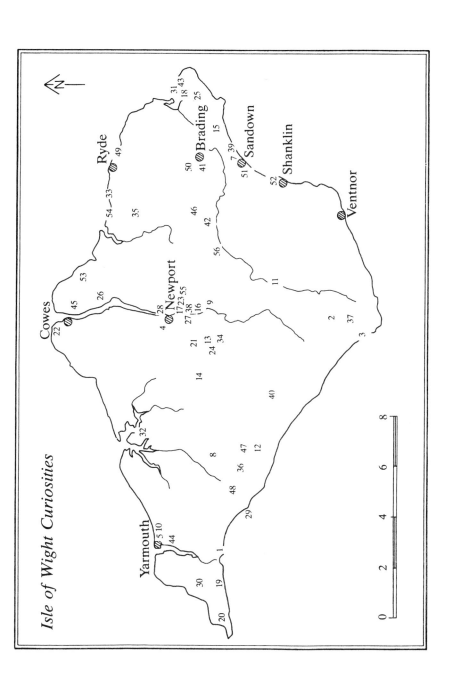

Isle of Wight Curiosities

1 A Cliff Accident

Position. Near cliff edge on Afton Down
Map Ref. SZ3527/8557
Access. Nearest road access is from the National Trust car park on the north side of the Military Road just east of Freshwater Bay. Cross the road to the south side, and the coastal footpath F35, and the obelisk, are in sight.

Note. A sad tale is told on this monument:

E.L.M. Aged 15
'He cometh forth like a flower and is cut down.
He fleeth also as a shadow and continueth not'.
Erected in remembrance of a most dear and only child who was suddenly removed into eternity by a fall from the adjacent cliff on the rocks beneath. 28th August 1846.
Reader prepare to meet thy God, for thou knowest not what a day may bring forth.

So the monument serves as a gentle reminder to later visitors that the cliffs can have their dangers. A local diarist records that in the 16th century several local people braved the cliff faces in the course of collecting samphire, a plant whose leaves are used in the making of pickles, and which tends to grow in such unreachable spots as cliff faces.

Until the 1930s the Island coastguards had wicker protective headgear rather like kendo helmets, for use in cliff rescue work when there was danger from falling rocks.

E. L. M.
AGED 16

THE COMETH FORTH
LIKE A FLOWER
AND IS CUT DOWN
HE FLEETH ALSO AS
A SHADOW AND
CONTINUETH NOT

2 The Two-faced Monument

Position. North end of St Catherine's Down
Map Ref. SZ4960/7880
Access. Driest and most scenic access over the down from the south.
From the Viewpoint Car Park on the A3055 just east of Blackgang
(Map Ref. SZ4910/7673) cross the road and take the steepish footpath
up to St Catherine's Oratory (the medieval lighthouse), and from there
along the down top.

Note. A prominent feature at the north end of St Catherine's Down is
the Hoy Monument, a tall stone column with a large finial sphere at the
top. It was built in 1814 by Michael Hoy, a merchant trading with
Russia, who lived at a house called the Hermitage on the eastern slope
of the down. The occasion was a visit to Britain by the Tsar Alexander I
of Russia, at that time – having just entered Paris in triumph at the head
of his armies – the lynchpin of the coalition against Napoleon. A small
inscription on white marble – recently reset, after extensive repairs, on
the north face of the plinth – reads:

In commemoration of the visit of his Majesty Alexander I, Emperor of all the
Russias, to Great Britain in 1814, in remembrance of many happy years
residence in his dominions this pillar was erected by Michael Hoy.

A later tablet though, on the south face of the column base, tells a
different tale. It was added by a subsequent owner of the land, and the
inscription reads:

This tablet was erected by William Henry Dawes late Lieutenant of H.M. 22
Regt in honor of those brave men of the allied armies who fell on the Alma at
Inkermann and at the siege of Sevastopol A.D. 1857.

Gone are the Russophile sentiments of Michael Hoy! The Crimean
War had changed all that.

The name of Hoy's nearby house, the Hermitage, may have less
to do with anchorites than with the Tsars' Hermitage Palace at St
Petersburg (later Petrograd, now Leningrad), though in this case the
Russian connection would have to go back as far as 1775 when the
name is first recorded on St Catherine's Down.

3 The Island's Wild West Village

Position. Blackgang Chine
Map Ref. SZ 4865/7652
Access. Turning off mini-roundabout on A3055, to Chine car park, and entrance at SZ4881/7675

Note. Blackgang Chine is not so much a theme park as a polythematic extravaganza. You can find almost anything there, from full-sized replicas of dinosaurs to a space craft.

In one of the farthest reaches from the entrance, down near the sea-shore, is Buffalo Creek with all the fun of the Wild West. It centres round the Last Chance Hotel (Meals $3; Whisky 5¢) with a gun-toting cow-puncher on the veranda propping up the front wall, while inside the inevitable endless card game is in progress. Near the U.S. Land Office is the Blacksmith and Livery Stables (Prop. Sam Hicks), and the offices of the Creek Gazette. Farther down the street is the Wells Fargo office with a coach standing outside, and the General Stores with the proprietor and his wife standing behind the counter. There is of course a Sheriff's Office with an uncomfortable-looking lock-up, enhanced however with a view down to the Buffalo Creek Railroad where a gleaming locomotive (no. 116) complete with cow-catcher at the front quite dwarfs a nearby covered wagon.

You might call this the town centre. In the outskirts are an Indian encampment with Indians, tepee, and totem pole; gold prospectors at their workings; and a log fort containing a children's play area. Also in the 'suburbs' is a trapper standing with his gun in front of a hut, apparently unaware of some bears appearing round the corner, clearly not paying a friendly social call. These hazards of frontier life may explain why Buffalo Creek has such an extensive graveyard; but the greatest hazard of all, and a real exercise in engineering, must have been to get that locomotive to its present position.

4 Newport's Blue Jenny

Position. 62 Crocker Street, Newport
Map Ref. SZ4981/8934

Note. In a niche over the door of a building in the eastern limb of
Crocker Street, Newport, is the carved figure of an 18th-century girl in
her school uniform, carrying a Bible and holding in her other hand a
George III penny – her church collection.

She reminds us that the charity school movement in the 18th century
was the first attempt to provide for the education of the children of the
poor in England. The Newport Blue School Foundation – a reference
to the characteristic blue dress of the children – was established in 1761
for the education of local girls. In 1764 a Newport couple, Benjamin
and Martha Cooke of Sea Street, bought a building in Lugley Street for
use as a school, which was to be regulated by the Minister of Newport
and six ladies.

There were twenty free places for girls, and six were also boarded
and lodged at the expense of the charity. Their education included
special training to fit them for domestic service. Every girl on leaving
was presented with suitable clothing, a Bible, and a prayer book; and if
she kept for one year the situation with which she had been provided,
she was rewarded with a gratuity of a sovereign.

Later the house at 62 Crocker Street was given to the charity, and the
school moved there, functioning until 1907 when it got into financial
difficulties. The building was sold, and after serving as a maternity
hospital for many years it was acquired by Hampshire County Council
and is now used to house the probation service.

The original carving of the 'Blue Jenny' figure over the door became
so weather-beaten that it was removed for safety to Carisbrooke Castle
Museum; and in 1980 the present replica figure, carved by Norman
Gaches, was substituted in the niche, thanks to the enthusiastic efforts
of the Newport Group of the Isle of Wight Society. Meanwhile the old
charity foundation still functions, and bursaries are awarded by the
Trustees.

5 An Innovative Castle Bastion

Position. Yarmouth Castle
Map Ref. SZ 3542/8976

Note. The early 1500s were interesting years in the history of
fortification, as military architects tried to adjust to the advent of
increasingly efficient cannons and gunpowder. So much theoretical
work was going on that when in the 1530s Henry VIII commissioned a
chain of coastal forts, including the Isle of Wight, he was served with a
motley assortment of designs. An example of the more old-fashioned
can still be seen in the half-moon bastion in front of Cowes Castle (now
the home of the Royal Yacht Squadron) giving a good spread of fire but
with such disadvantages as occasional blind spots uncovered from
elsewhere on the defensive perimeter.

   The newest idea, thought up by the Italians, was the arrowhead
bastion which allowed good defensive cover. Yarmouth Castle, built in
the 1540s, has one of these at the south-east corner covering the two
landward faces of the fort, and it is certainly among the earliest
examples of its kind in Britain. It is now partly masked by the
neighbouring George Hotel but it can be seen from the north end of
Pier Street, just by the pier entrance. When the castle – in the care of
English Heritage – is open you can go inside the bastion and examine
the cannon embrasures with their overhead smoke vents.

   From the town square, incidentally, you can see the original
entrance gateway, splendidly surmounted by the Henry VIII coat of
arms, of the formerly moated castle. The gateway now opens on to the
lawn of the hotel, but the modern entrance to the castle is round the
corner in Quay Street.

*Yarmouth Castle. The protruding arrowhead bastion is to the left of the entrance
gate.*

Yarmouth Castle.

6 The Island's Special Butterfly

Position. Various, along the southern cliffs of the Island.

Note. The Glanville Fritillary is a butterfly found nowhere in mainland Britain, and in the Island only along a narrow strip near the southern cliffs. It is a rarity but it is hard to say why. The ribwort plantain on which the butterfly lays its eggs is a quite common plant, and the hatched caterpillars seem able to stand quite cold winters, lurking in ground-hugging vegetation. It may be that the slightly earlier spring season on the Island encourages the pupation of the caterpillars, a process ending in late May and in June with the next wave of these attractive butterflies with their diaper black and orange colouring.

The name Fritillary was first recorded in 1583 as being applied by a French druggist, Noel Capperon, to the flower with similar markings 'quod eius arealae versicolores fritillum quodam-modo aemulentur' ('because its chequered spots in a certain way resemble a fritillus', that is, a dice-box). Gerard's *Herball* in 1597 though, referring to the same flower, observes: 'It hath been called Frittillaria, of the table or boord upon which men plaie at chesse, which square checkers the flower doth very much resemble, some thinking that it' (that is, the chess board) 'was named Frittillus'. Anyway the name latched also on to the butterflies with such markings; and the Glanville part of the name derives from a naturalist of the late 1700s, Lady Glanville, whose collection of insects was found to include the Island's own butterfly, now adopted as the emblem of the I.W. Natural History and Archaeological Society.

As the Glanville lives near the cliff tops, tread carefully for your sake and for the butterfly's!

7 An Old Inhabitant: Bernissartensis

Position. Sandown
Map Ref. SZ 6015/8439

Note. The Museum of Isle of Wight Geology in the upper floor of the County Library's branch library at Sandown is restricted in space but manages to show some quite large specimens; old ones too, very old.

One interesting recent discovery now on exhibition consists of the fossil remains of a dinosaur, *Iguanodon Bernissartensis*, recovered from the cliff at Atherfield in 1976 and 1978. It lived about 115 million years ago, but in a landscape that would be quite strange to us today. The Isle of Wight was then a thing of the future, as was the English Channel. These creatures occupied a quite different land, the wide valley of a north-flowing river. There were no people around at that time – just as well, for *Bernissartensis* was not the sort of creature to meet in a dark valley. It wouldn't eat you, for it was a herbivore, but with the best intentions it might still squash you flat!

Incidentally the tooth of a carnivorous dinosaur was found with the Iguanodon remains, but the palaeontologists examining the deposit resisted the temptation to script a gripping scenario of sudden death in the Cretaceous period, for the tooth was derived from another stratum and its owner lived at a different period. Just a million years or so.

The Mounted skeleton of the Atherfield dinosaur.

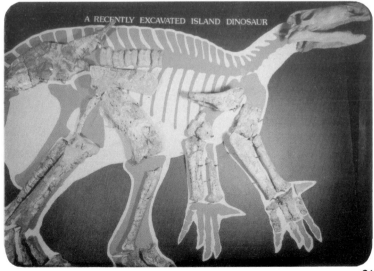

8 The Big Gun of Calbourne

Position. On B3401 west of Calbourne
Map Ref. SZ 4141/8678

Note. At a transport history conference one enthusiast, offering his
address to another, said: 'Do call and see me if you are ever in
Cambridge; you can't miss my house – it's the one with a steam roller
on the front lawn'.

You could say much the same of Calbourne Water Mill and Museum
of Rural Life – it's the one with a 38-ton gun at the roadside. There are
two smaller gun barrels lying beside it, but they are dwarfed in
comparison.

This fearsome firearm was one of four that used to be part of the
armament at Cliff End Battery near Colwell Bay at the west of the
Island. On the mainland side of the Solent's western entrance Hurst
Castle was similarly equipped to help in protecting the naval base at
Portsmouth. The guns were 19 feet 2 inches long, with a rifled bore of
12½ inches, and muzzle loading – quite a ceremony it must have been
to fire them. They were in fact never fired in action, though a test firing
in 1878 did some spectacular damage to Cliff End Fort! The guns were
taken out of service at the beginning of this century.

The mill itself is a nice example of a water mill in working order, with
its overshot wheel; and it stands in pleasantly landscaped grounds, with
waterfowl and peacocks to add tone.

9 The Man who Listened to the Earth Trembling

Position. At the side of A3020 south of Newport (see *Note* below)
Map Ref. SZ 5035/8795

Note. Professor John Milne (1850-1913) was a geologist and mineralogist. After studies of geology and mining in England and Germany, in 1875 he was appointed Professor of those subjects in Imperial College, Tokio. It was typical of his enterprise and enquiring spirit that he chose to travel out there through Siberia and Mongolia, an eleven-month journey full of scares and excitements.

Then, on the first night after his arrival in Tokio, something happened that changed the whole course of his career. It was a

Professor John Milne shortly before his death.

common event for the Japanese: an earthquake. For Milne however it was the start of a new scientific interest. With the co-operation of the Japanese government he began the systematic study of seismology, and for fifteen years he was secretary of the Seismological Society of Japan which he had taken the lead in founding.

When he returned to England in 1895, now with a Japanese government pension and also the award of the Order of the Rising Sun, he continued his research here, based on his laboratory at Shide on the south-east fringe of Newport. Here with his Japanese wife – daughter of the abbot of Ganjo-ji, Hakodate – he received a stream of fellow-scientists who came to benefit from his findings. It was here too that he developed the horizontal pendulum seismograph, an instrument of great sensitivity in detecting and amplifying ground shocks.

Recently, thanks to the enthusiasm of two local science historians – Patrick Nott and Leslie Herbert-Gustar – the work of this pioneer scientist has been recognized in the Island, and on 14 March 1974 His Excellency the Japanese Ambassador came to plant a flowering tree *Prunus Kanzan* and to unveil a plaque from Tokio University in honour of this 'father of seismology'. This is opposite the site of Milne's former laboratory: on the west verge of Blackwater Road, A3020, near a south-facing official sign reading 'Welcome to Newport, County Town of the Isle of Wight'.

10 The Strange Tale of a Statue

Position. St James's Church, Yarmouth
Map Ref. SZ3548/8967

Note. The Holmes chapel, an early addition to the south of the chancel
in Yarmouth church, is dominated by the tomb and large white marble
statue of Sir Robert Holmes. A naval commander in the best cavalier
tradition, he had served under Prince Rupert in the Civil War. After
the restoration of Charles II in 1660 Holmes took service with the
Royal African Company, and the English guinea coin is believed to

have taken its name from Holmes's gold plunder from West Africa.

In 1668 he was appointed as Captain and Governor of the Isle of Wight – the first to hold a royal warrant for the title of Governor – and he held this appointment for 24 stormy years, including the 1688 revolution, until his death in 1692; which brings us to his impressive tomb and statue.

There are two versions of the statue story. One, recorded a few years after Holmes's death, records that Holmes retrieved the 'marble' – presumably ready carved – from the wreck on the Island coast of a ship bound for France, and thriftily put it on one side for his own use. According to the more colourful version the statue, with its face yet unmodelled, was meant to be a figure of King Louis XIV of France. The sculptor, travelling with it, survived the wreck and was ordered by Holmes to complete it with his, Holmes's face. The size and opulence of the statue, and the brazenness of Holmes's alleged action, both make the story seem quite plausible. Whatever the truth, the monument has impressed or irritated visitors ever since. Celia Fiennes wrote, after seeing it in the 1690s: 'Sir Robert Holmes . . . is buried where is his statue cutt in length in white marble in the Church and railed in with Iron Grates, he was raised from nothing and an imperious Governor and what he scrap'd together was forced to leave to his Nephew and base daughter haveing no other, and they have set up this stately Monument which cost a great deal'.

11 The Buried Milestone in Bow Bridge

Position. Between Rookley and Godshill

Map Ref. SZ5238/8269

Note. On the A3020 from Rookley, just before a right-hand bend in to north Godshill, is a piece of Georgian England: a hump bridge over the tiny River Yar.

It begins to tell its own tale. An inscribed stone in the inner face of the south wall reads:

ERECTED IN THE YEAR 1769. TO NEWPORT QUAY . . .

and here we lose it. As the road surface has been made up over the years it has gradually submerged the helpful but rather quaint milestone information.

The stone in fact goes on to give the mileage north to Newport Quay – the harbour at Newport was then very busy and bustling – and south to . . . Appuldurcombe. The strange thing about this is that Appuldurcombe was not even a village; it was a stately house recently built in Palladian style on the site of a Tudor manor house. Its mention

The milestone, Bow Bridge.

thus tells us about the author of the inscription and the builder of the bridge. Sir Richard Worsley had succeeded as seventh baronet in 1768 at the age of seventeen, and his pride in Appuldurcombe is clear from the Bow Bridge inscription. He became active in Island affairs as well as being a notable antiquary and historian, and his house became a fine museum of paintings and antiquities. It survives today as a shell, having been finished off by a land mine in the 1939-45 war, but is in the care of English Heritage and is open to visitors.

The old railway line from Newport to Ventnor used to pass over the road immediately to the south-east of Bow Bridge, hence the present 90-degree bend to the right just after the site of the now vanished railway and bridge.

Take care in looking at the road bridge inscription. The bridge is not wide, and the traffic usually busy!

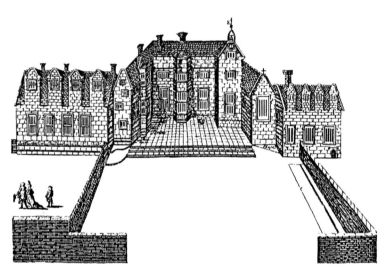

Elizabethan Appuldurcombe, demolished by Robert Worsley in about 1720.

The 18th century house of the Worsleys at Appuldurcombe.

12 The Mystery of the Carved Ships

Position. Brighstone
Map Ref. SZ4255/8375

Note. Take the Calbourne Road north out of the centre of Brighstone
starting with Moortown Lane, and soon after the junction with Upper
Lane you pass the little lane to Coombe Farm on your right; almost
immediately on your left, at the roadside, is a small barn built of large
chalk blocks. This is where to stop and begin counting ships: big ones,
little ones, ships with sails furled, others with sails set – all gouged out
as line drawings in the workable chalk.

   The flotilla you are looking at is part of a large fleet of ship carvings
on outside and inside walls of cottages in the Island. There are some
stray examples inland, but they are found mainly along the south coast,
and especially near the south-west coast of the Island. The types of
ships illustrated date chiefly from the late 18th and early 19th century;
and because this was the golden age of smuggling in the Island it has
been suggested that the ships were some kind of mark used by the
smugglers in their trade, for delivery to individual houses or for
collection of contraband from secret stores. In that case, though, this
barn at Rock near Brighstone rather overdid the number of its secret
signs. It seems more likely that local fishermen and other sailors,
finding that their homes were potentially carvable, indulged in the idle
entertainment of the modern graffito artist, and took for their subject
the theme they lived with – ships and the sea. Although the sheer
number of carvings seems special to the island, stray examples are
known from Romney Marsh in Kent, from East Anglia, and indeed
from farther afield. An old Christian church at Trabzon (formerly
Trebizond) in eastern Turkey has its walls full of carved sailing ships,
reportedly drawn by visiting sailors; and Spike Milligan published in
Country Life in January 1981 a carving of *The Dash*, an emigrant ship
of 1840, on the wall of St James's Church at Blackiston near Adelaide,
Australia.

13 The Oldest Organ in Britain

Position. Carisbrooke Castle Museum
Map Ref. SZ4857/8779

Note. This is not a church organ. Modest in size, it was the kind of instrument that would have graced one of the richer Tudor houses for use in its domestic music. It lives now at Carisbrooke Castle, in the museum there, and it arrived in 1937 presented to H.R.H. Princess Beatrice – the youngest daughter of Queen Victoria, the longest-serving Governor of the Island, and incidentally the last governor to live at the castle – by the Islanders to celebrate her 80th birthday.

The story of the instrument fades quickly into the mists of history. It was known to have been on the Island, in the possession of a family at Bonchurch, in the late 1800s, and then was acquired by an owner on the mainland. It carried with it a tradition – which remains unsupported by contemporary documents – that it had been played at Carisbrooke by Princess Elizabeth, daughter of Charles I, during her brief imprisonment there in 1650. For this reason Princess Beatrice hankered to see it back at Carisbrooke, and the Island responded by buying and presenting it.

Apart from the Princess Elizabeth connection though, the organ itself is a historical and musical treasure, and one that spans frontiers. It was made in 1602 – the date is carved on the front of the case – apparently in Flanders, for the case has an incised text in Flemish, from Psalm 150, verse 4: 'Praise him with stringed instruments and organs'. Its first owner though was the Scottish Earl of Montrose, whose heraldry and monogram is included in the carved decoration of the pipe case, and some of the stoppers in the flue pipes are carved as Scottish thistles. There are two main stops: a stopped diapason, and a flute; and a reed stop, called a regal, was an afterthought addition apparently by the original builders. The untempered tuning still reproduces the original Renaissance sound of the instrument.

14 The Haunt without a Ghost

Position. Near Carisbrooke
Map Ref. SZ4640/8792

Note. A mile west of Carisbrooke on the B3401 to Calbourne, just past
the Blacksmith's Arms is a turning to the north with the intriguing
name of Betty Haunt Lane. This tells us not that there has been a ghost
here but that there used to be a hunting park; for a 'haunt' was the
name used for a place where deer came to be fed.

It looks less like a park now – just open farm land; but look at a map
and you will see a cluster of names like Great Park, Park Place Farm,
Green Park Farm, and Park Green Farm. Domesday Book in 1086
mentions 'parco regis' (the King's park), and a document of 1364 refers
to the 'King's chace of Parkehurste' implying that the old Parkhurst
Forest – originally much more extensive than the modern plantation of
that name – took in the Carisbrooke Park area. By the 16th century this
was an impaled park, showing as such on maps of the period, and its
eastern boundary was virtually on the line of Betty Haunt Lane. Being
a royal park, the use of it was a perquisite of the Island Captains who
were appointed by the Crown, and they sometimes lived at the lodge
there, rather than at Carisbrooke Castle. Sir George Carey, who was
Captain from 1583 to 1603, subscribed some of his letters from 'the
Parke'. It was there that he entertained the local gentry to hunting
parties; and it was there that he nearly met a violent death at such a
party when his sister Lady Hoby accidentally (one hopes!) fired her
crossbow at him. Carey's horse reared just at that moment and took the
bolt in its own head.

So much for the haunt. Why Betty? No one is really sure, but one
local historian has suggested that it could be a dialect corruption of
'between', for the present lane is on the boundary between the manors
of Swainston and Alvington.

15 The Remains of a Medieval Lunch Break

Position. Church of St John the Baptist, Yaverland
Map Ref. SZ 6040/8595
Access. On B3395 from Sandown to Bembridge

Note. The charming little medieval church at Yaverland blends
perfectly with the Tudor manor house next to it. The house incidentally
was the scene of an almost rags to riches story in the 16th century when
German Richards, having made a profitable marriage, invested this
new wealth in a brewery next to Brading church, and by this means
proceeded to make his fortune on naval victualling. He futher invested
some of this money in buying an interest in Yaverland manor, and his
son finally bought the house outright.

The delightful church has a particularly fine south door of the
Norman period. The building into which the doorway admitted you
was previously even smaller than it is today, for the tiny north aisle was
added in 1889. It was in the course of this construction that the pieces of
a medieval earthenware cooking pot were found lying near the footings
of the Norman north wall. The pot – presumably one used by the
original church builders – has been restored and is now displayed on a
bracket at the west end of the nave: the surviving remains of a medieval
lunch break.

The name Yaverland is an ancient one, and its Saxon roots mean
'land where the boars were kept'.

16 Bath Night for the Romans

Position. Cypress Road, Newport
Map Ref. SZ5013/8852
Access. Open daily (except Sat) 10.00 to 4.30 from Good Friday to the
end of September. Wide road for parking.

Note. Cypress Road on the southern skirts of Newport seems at first
glance to comprise a normal line of houses; but towards the lower
eastern end, as the road slopes down towards the river valley, is a
structure set slightly back from the road. It contains the Newport
Roman villa, found in the 1920s during construction of a garage,
excavated, and later given by the Millgate family to the I.W. County
Council, whose Museums Service now cares for it.

It is a corridor villa – a range of rooms with two end wings and a
linking corridor veranda – built in the second century A.D. and of fairly
standard pattern.

The hypocaust heating, Newport Roman villa, with the steam bath on the right.

What is special about it is the exceptionally well-preserved range of bath rooms in the west wing, surely one of the best examples in Britain. Some parts of the floors have not survived, obligingly giving a cutaway model effect showing the function of the hypocaust heating; for all the warm-room floors are suspended on pillars of tile, leaving room for the hot fumes from the external furnace entry to flow. The nearer to the stokehole, the hotter the room. We enter this blend of sauna and Turkish bath by the apodyterium where bathers undressed; then through the frigidarium or cold room, to the tepidarium (warm room) and finally the caldarium (hot room) where the bather would be massaged with oil and then scraped clean with a kind of squeegee called a strigil; and the hot room has a real Turkish bath alcove where splashed water would generate plenty of steam, because the hot-air flue there runs inside the walls as well as under the floor. After all this came the agony of returning for a splash in the plunge bath of the frigidarium – and this bath still has its original lead waste pipe. The Romans too, like our house guests, tended to spend hours in the bathroom – but there *was* more room!

Monument to Princess Elizabeth, daughter of Charles I, Newport.

17 Burial of a Princess

Position. St Thomas's Church, Newport
Map Ref. SZ4998/8915

Note. In Newport parish church, at the east end of the north aisle, is a
Victorian monument to Elizabeth, daughter of Charles I; and thereby
hangs a tale.

When Charles I spent his year as a prisoner on the Island in 1647-8
only three of his immediate family remained in England – his children
James, Henry, and Elizabeth; and James (the future King James II)
made his escape abroad, disguised as a girl, during that year. Shortly
before his execution in Whitehall on 30 January 1649 Charles had a
tearful meeting with Henry and Elizabeth, in the course of which
Henry promised his father that he would not allow Parliament to put
him on the throne while his two elder brothers, Charles and James
were alive.

The death of the King and the start of a republic seemed to mean
open-ended imprisonment for the two royal children; and in due
course, in August 1650, they too were lodged in Carisbrooke Castle,
the scene of their father's solitary captivity. For the ten-year-old Henry
it was the beginning of a long stay, ending in 1653 when he was released
to join his family in France. Elizabeth though survived barely three
weeks. Caught in the rain out on the castle's bowling alley, she became
very ill and died on 8 September, aged nearly fifteen; and she was
buried with little ceremony in Newport church. Then, during some
building repairs in 1793, the small vault with her coffin was found, and
was then marked with a brass plate. Finally when the church was
rebuilt in the 1850s Queen Victoria commissioned a new monument for
the tomb, with a carved figure of the dead princess by Baron
Marochetti: a more fitting monument for the church's only royal
burial.

18 Maker of the Island's own Aircraft

Position. Churchyard of Holy Trinity, Bembridge
Map Ref. SZ6436/8822

Note. Working around the skies in different parts of the world today is
a graceful aircraft called the Islander – an elegantly outlined high-wing
monoplane with tricycle undercarriage. In an age of elaborate
technology, when an aircraft seems to cost an average national debt to
acquire or maintain, the Islander has an almost Palladian simplicity and
harmony of design; and it has met a real need in parts of the world
where distances are vast and operational budgets limited.

   Its designer John Forester Richard Britten seemed marked for a
career at sea when he went to the Royal Naval College at Dartmouth,
but his path took some unexpected turns. For three years after the
Second World War he was managing director of his family's cinema
and theatre business; then in 1954 with N. D. Norman he founded
Britten-Norman Limited based at Bembridge airport. Here, as joint
managing director, he was able to exploit his skill in aeronautical
design. His work in developing the Islander aircraft was recognized by
the award of a C.B.E. in 1970, and in 1976 – the year before his death –
he served as High Sheriff of the Isle of Wight.

   His gravestone in Bembridge churchyard, near the north-east corner
of the church, describes him as 'Designer and Builder of Aeroplanes';
and engraved near the top of the stone are the flowing lines of his
masterpiece, the Islander.

An "Islander" at Bembridge airport.

JOHN BRITTEN
BORN MAY 27TH 1928
DIED JULY 7TH 1977
DESIGNER AND BUILDER
OF
AEROPLANES
EVELYN ZOË RHODES BRITTEN
1898 — 1980

19 Monument to a Poet Laureate

Position. Tennyson Down, west of Freshwater Bay
Map Ref. SZ3250/8533
Access. Footpath from Freshwater Bay, over Tennyson Down. Start near the Freshwater Bay car park, on the south-western side of Gate Lane next to the public convenience. A different footpath taking a more northerly track over the down begins by the bus shelter near St Agnes Church (the only thatched church on the Island) farther up Gate Lane opposite its junction with Blackbridge Road.

Note. It was the remote peacefulness of the Island that drew Alfred Tennyson to settle at Farringford in 1853. He came at a stage in his career when he was achieving some critical acclaim – succeeding as Poet Laureate on the death of Wordsworth in 1850 – and increasingly wide sales of his works. Popularity was all very well, but Tennyson found that his poetry flowed best from a tranquil setting. There was as yet no branch railway from Brockenhurst to Lymington, and the steam ferry service to Yarmouth was recently established and still fitful. By day Tennyson could walk on the neighbouring down or enjoy the view out into the Channel from his grounds; and at night he could pursue his interest in astronomy – he was much interested in the theories of Laplace – from an observatory platform on the Farringford roof. These conditions agreed with him and he wrote contentedly. His first major work after coming to the Island, *Maud*, though savaged by some of the critics, sold so well that he was able to buy the freehold of Farringford, which he had previously leased.

His presence at Freshwater drew a widening circle of notable visitors there – Benjamin Jowett, Edward Lear, Sir John Millais, Sir Arthur Sullivan, F. D. Maurice, Charles Darwin, and Prince Albert. He also attracted increasing numbers of sightseers, whose presence became so oppressive that in 1869 he acquired another, quieter house at Aldworth near Haslemere where he could retreat in the summer season, though still keeping his base at Farringford.

After his death in 1892 the great, marble Maltese cross was put up on the down where he had walked, and which now bears his name, on the former site of the old Nodes signal beacon which had signalled ancient invasion threats. 'In memory of Alfred Lord Tennyson', the inscription reads, 'this Cross is raised as a beacon to sailors by the people of Freshwater and other friends in England and America'.

20 A Cradle of Radio

Position. In the car park of the Needles Pleasure Park, Alum Bay
Map Ref. SZ3069/8549
Access. B3322 leading into car park.

Note. This is a place of pilgrimage for those enthusiasts of the history of
radio, though the only visible trace of Marconi is the commemorative
stone with its set of four narrative plaques. It was on this spot on the
cliff above Alum Bay that Marconi carried out his early experiments in
long-distance radio telegraphy.

What he did was to take Hertz's spark transmitter circuit, developed
in the 1880s, and refine the equipment by actual field experiment. He
was a practical man, taking up where the physicists left off. After a
preliminary canter at his native Bologna in 1894, he came to England
and, in collaboration with William Preece of the post office, he began
field experiments first on Salisbury Plain and then across the Bristol
Channel.

In 1897 he came to the Isle of Wight and here at Alum Bay a
transmitting station was built under the personal supervision of
Marconi, by his assistant George Kemp. The station, which Marconi
described as the world's 'first permanent wireless station', was
completed on 5 December and Marconi now began a series of tests
monitoring the range of signal reception by a tug at varying distances,
first in Alum Bay and then extending out to Bournemouth and then to
Poole – a range of 18 miles. Later the signal was successfully received
by ships 40 miles out to sea.

Marconi observed the effects of various heights of aerial, of earthing
one side of the spark gap, and of using different designs of Branly's
coherer which operated the receiving relay. This incidentally allowed
the actual printing out of the received Morse signal by an automatic
pen on a moving paper tape.

The great, the good, and the famous began to make the pilgrimage to
this scene of wonders at Alum Bay. On 3 June 1898 Lord Kelvin sent
from this station the first radio telegram for which payment was made;
and on 15 November 1899 the first newspaper ever produced at sea –
the *Transatlantic Times* – was transmitted from the Needles station and
printed on the American liner *St Paul*, then 36 miles away.

Transmissions here continued until 26 May 1900, after which the
station was dismantled to be moved to a new site at Knowles Farm,
Niton, at the southern tip of the Island. The passage of the great aerial

THIS STONE
MARKS THE SITE OF THE
NEEDLES
WIRELESS TELEGRAPH STATION
WHERE
GUGLIELMO MARCONI
AND HIS BRITISH COLLABORATORS
CARRIED OUT FROM
6TH DECEMBER 1897
TO 26TH MAY 1900
A SERIES OF EXPERIMENTS
WHICH CONSTITUTED SOME OF
THE MORE IMPORTANT PHASES
OF THEIR EARLIER PIONEER
WORK IN THE DEVELOPMENT OF
WIRELESS COMMUNICATION
OF ALL KINDS.

mast through the intervening country lanes is now part of local folklore! At Niton, with the further refinement of a tuned circuit, there were even more impressive results.

Marconi had his excitements on the Island in addition to the thrill of radio experimenting. He was invited to set up a radio link at Osborne House for Queen Victoria; and there, in due course, he was contentedly prowling around the grounds choosing a suitable place for his aerial mast when he was jumped on by zealous police guards, under the impression that he was a potential Fenian assassin.

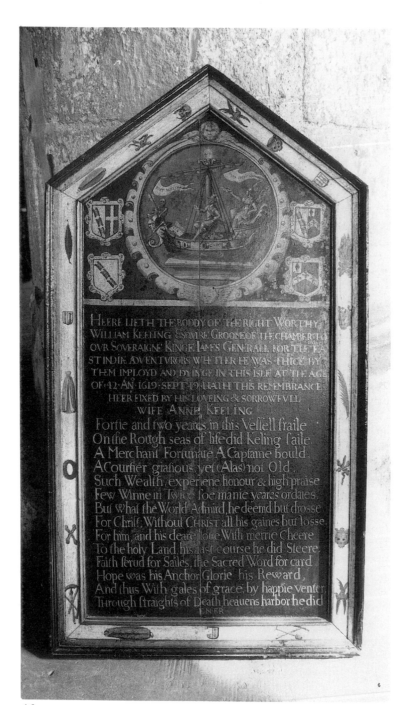

21 A Sinbad of Shakespeare's Time

Position. St Mary's Church, Carisbrooke
Map Ref. SZ4857/8826

Note. In the north-east corner of Carisbrooke Church, near the
sanctuary rail, is a commemorative panel of a man who after a life of
great adventure ended his days in the relative quiet of the Isle of Wight.
William Keeling (1577-1619) was a courtier – groom of the chamber to
King James I – but above all a sea captain. As agent of the East India
Company he made three voyages – the last two as commander – to what
is now Indonesia. In 1609 in the course of the second voyage he
discovered the Cocos Keeling Islands, a coral island group in the Indian
Ocean south of Sumatra. Finally he sought a peaceful retirement in the
Isle of Wight with two Crown appointments there, as Captain of Cowes
Castle and as Keeper of the Park, a royal hunting enclosure just to the
west of Carisbrooke, where he and his wife Anne lived.

After his death on 19 September 1619 his widow commissioned the
charming memorial panel now in the church. One of his Island friends,
Sir John Oglander, later described him as 'a worthie man', and the
memorial conveys something of this esteem. Within a funerary border,
and flanked by family coats of arms, is a roundel with an allegorical
picture of Keeling aboard a ship with a skeleton as figurehead and with
Fame in the poop holding a laurel crown towards Keeling. Flying
pennants carry a Latin legend reading 'After death, Fame follows'. In
front of Keeling is an open Bible with the words 'Verbum Dei' ('the
Word of God'). The Christian monogram surmounts the picture, and
the symbolism is picked out by the word 'Caro' ('flesh') on the ship's
gunwale.

The inscription below ends with a piece of verse using a typically
Jacobean figure of Keeling making his last sea voyage, to the Holy
Land: 'Faith servd for Sailes, the Sacred Word for card, Hope was his
Anchor, Glorie his Reward'.

22 The Castle Prison of a Poet

Position. Cowes Castle
Map Ref. SZ 4940/9656
Access. To seaward bastion only, from the Parade. The rest of the
Castle now houses the Royal Yacht Squadron.

Note. It was not by choice that Sir William Davenant came to the Isle of
Wight. He was a prolific poet and playwright during the reign of
Charles I, much favoured at Court, and when the Civil War began in
1642 he took the royalist side. As Charles's forces began to fall apart,
Davenant fled to Paris, and he was still in France at the time of the
King's execution.

In 1650 Charles's wife Henrietta Maria, who also had fled to her
native France some years before, sent Davenant on a mission to the
American colonies; but he was intercepted by an English ship not far
off the French coast, and brought as a prisoner to Cowes Castle. This
small fort, now – much altered – housing the Royal Yacht Squadron,
had been built in the 1530s by Henry VIII and its first recorded use as a
prison, in 1642 had not been an outstanding success because all its
doors were found to be without locks or bolts. Things were better
ordered when Davenant arrived, and under lock and key he settled

Cowes Castle in the 18th century.

Cowes Castle, now the home of the Royal Yacht Squadron.

down to literary work. In France he had begun writing a romantic epic, set in Verona, called *Gondibert*. It was in the same metre as the much later Gray's *Elegy* – this in itself was nothing new, for Spenser had used it for his *Faerie Queene*, but an unusual feature was the use of short, four-line stanzas, not easy to adapt to a lengthy epic. And lengthy *Gondibert* was: Davenant had already written two books in France, and now for nine months at Cowes toiled over Book Three. On 20 October 1650, half way through it, he wrote: 'tis high time to strike sail and cast anchor (though I have run but half my course) when at the helme I am threatened with Death who, though he can visit us but once, seems troublesome; and even in the innocent may beget such a gravity as diverts the musick of verse'. Well might he worry. He was soon moved to the Tower, with a trial and execution pending; but he finally escaped with his life, reportedly at the urging of John Milton – a case of poets sticking together; and *Gondibert*, having reached some 7,000 lines, was never completed.

23 A Stuart Pulpit

Position. St Thomas's Church, Newport
Map Ref. SZ4998/8915

Note. Newport parish church is a deceptive building. It looks and is mid-Victorian, but inside are some of the features from the medieval building it replaced.

One of the most splendid and unmissable of these is an elaborate pulpit complete with tester or sounding board, given by a local merchant Stephen March in about 1631. The outer face is covered with carving, fourteen panels of it, in two tiers, The upper tier contains the three theological virtues Faith, Hope, and Charity; and the four cardinal virtues Justice, Prudence, Temperance, and Fortitude. Below are the seven liberal arts and sciences Grammar, Logic, Rhetoric, Music, Arithmetic, Geometry, and Astronomy. Under the headboard is a golden dove representing the Holy Spirit, and this was discreetly packed away by the Puritans under Cromwell, to bide its time and fly again after the Restoration in 1660. The remaining doveless pulpit must have been still too ornate for Puritan taste, but it could hardly be removed because of the Reformation emphasis on preaching.

Look for the text from Isaiah 58, verse 1 painted round the edge of the headboard: 'Cry aloud and spare not: life up thy voice like a trumpet'. One minister who failed to do so indeed lost his job. In September 1653 William Martin was dismissed by the town corporation – who did the hiring and firing of their ministers – 'they assigning the cause of their dissent to be the lowness and weakness of his voice, whereof very few of the congregation could hear his doctrine or receive benefit by his public ministry'.

Wihtgar's gravestone.

24 Wihtgar Returns to Carisbrooke

Position. Carisbrooke Castle; in moat, next to tea room
Map Ref. SZ4851/8780
Access. Summer season only, when tea room is open. Just inside outer
gate, turn left through wooden gates opposite ticket kiosk.

Note. If you visit Carisbrooke Castle in the summer when the tea room
in the moat is open you will be able to see a true curiosity at the foot of
the adjoining castle bank. This is a large gravestone with the legend:

In memory of WIHTGAR the beautiful St Bernard dog of the late Captain
Markland formerly custodian of Carisbrooke Castle and the faithful companion
of Mr Markland till he died at Amherst on the 16th August 1899

Captain Markland applied his professional skill in military science to
good effect in his study of the history of the castle. He published in the
Proceedings of the Hampshire Field Club a conjectural restoration of
the castle in the 14th century, and recent excavations have shown how
sound his intuition was. But let us return to the dog: how did he acquire
his unusual name?

   The entry for 544 A.D. in the Anglo-Saxon Chronicle reads: 'This
year Wihtgar died, and they buried him in Wihtgaraburh': meaning
'Wihtgar's fortress'; meaning – Camden added in the 16th century –
Carisbrooke. Alas, the place-name etymologists assure us that
Wihtgaraburh will not corrupt into Carisbrooke; the molecules just
won't mix. One historian though has come up with an elegant solution.
He suggested that Wihtgar was indeed buried at Wihtgaraburh which
just happened to coincide with the present site of Carisbrooke. Why
not? It is nice to think that both the Wihtgars – two-footed and four-
footed – have found the same resting place.

25 The Island's only Windmill

Position. Mill Road, Bembridge
Map Ref. SZ6399/8748

Note. You might say that the Bembridge windmill is not really a curiosity. It is a fairly typical 'tower' or 'cap' mill of the early 1700s; but it is undeniably the only one left – and there were never a lot anyway! The Island is watermill rather than windmill country, not for shortage of breezes but because there is plenty of chalk country, and chalk is a generous aquifer that can usually keep the mill leats flowing with water.

Bembridge was a working windmill until just before the First World War. Until 1897 it produced flour, meal, and cattle feed; from then on, only cattle feed, and work finally stopped after the harvest of 1913. In the First World War the mill served as a store, and as a shelter for the Volunteer Reserve on night duty. Between the wars some limited restoration work was done, and in the Second World War history repeated itself when the Army used the mill as a lookout, and the local Dad's Army made it their headquarters.

After the War the mill was given to the National Trust and a devoted band of enthusiasts set to work to restore it to much of its former glory. This was an uphill job because two of the sweeps were destroyed in the hurricane of October 1987; but now it is all together again. Start your tour outside, with a look at the steering mechanism for the cap and sweeps; then it's best to climb to the top and browse your way downwards, following the sequence from the raw grain to the sifted flour. The various processes are well labelled and described.

26 The Yachtsman who Saved Lives of Wartime Aircrews

Position. Churchyard of St Mildred's, Whippingham
Map Ref. SZ5111/9367

Note. On the north side of Whippingham churchyard is the grave of the yachtsman and naval architect Uffa Fox (1898-1972) who put his stamp particularly on the design of smaller racing yachts. One of his most impressive productions was the international 14-footer *Avenger*, a planing dinghy with a hull of flattened V section instead of the more conventional round one, giving such a startling turn of speed that in 57 races (in 1928) it won 52 firsts, 2 seconds, and 3 thirds.

To return to the gravestone at Whippingham: illustrated on it, without comment, is a lifeboat drifting down suspended from three parachutes. This airborne lifeboat was perhaps Uffa's supreme invention, and it saved the lives of many aircrew during the Second World War. A twenty-foot plywood boat, it was designed to be carried folded in the rescue aircraft but would be automatically unfolded by the parachutes as it was dropped. It was self-righting and self-baling, equipped with an engine and fuel for a thousand miles, food for a month, and able to carry 25 men in shelter over thousands of miles of stormy ocean (it could travel under sail as well as power). Many on the Island and elsewhere remember with pleasure Uffa's exuberant personality and his tireless repertoire of sea shanties; and many airmen who never knew him still live to thank him for that invention illustrated on his grave.

27 Monument to a Boy Chimney Sweep

Position. Church Litten, Newport, near entrance to Lord Louis
Library
Map Ref. SZ4999/8887

Note. In the early 1800s the usual way of sweeping any substantial
chimney was to send a little boy up it, brushing the soot as he climbed.
One of these climbing boys was Valentine Gray a nine-year-old pauper
from Alverstoke who went to work for a Newport sweep, a Mr Davis.
One day the boy was found dead in his sleeping quarters, an
outbuilding of a house in Pyle Street. A surgeon who examined the
body found that it was a mass of bruises, and that the cause of death
was a severe blow to the head. There was a prolonged inquest, and
eventually Davis and his wife were imprisoned for manslaughter.

The public compassion for the boy's fate was expressed in the
inscription on the monument which now stands in Litten Park:

To the memory of VALENTINE GRAY the little sweep
Interred January the 5th A.D. 1822 in the 10th year of his age

In testimony of the general feeling for suffering innocence this monument is
erected by public subscription

From this and other abuses the pressure of opinion on Parliament built
up, and after abortive or ineffective Acts in 1840 and 1864 (the latter
prompted by Charles Kingsley's *Water Babies*) Lord Shaftesbury got a
remedial Act through in 1875: too late for Valentine, whose monument
now stands in mute reproach of former cruelty.

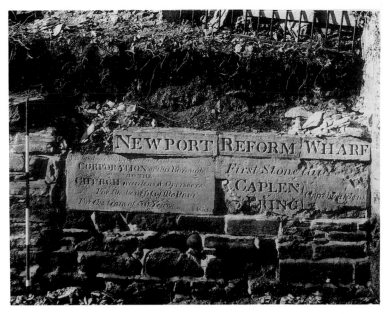

The Reform Wharf inscription before removal from the Quay.

28 The Wharf that became part of a Bridge

Position. Newport
Map Ref. SZ5029/8923

Note. In the wall of Coppin's Bridge over the River Medina at the bottom of Newport High Street are some stones with the engraved inscription:

NEWPORT REFORM WHARF
The land on which this wharf is erected was given
by the Corporation of this Borough to the Church Wardens
& Overseers for the benefit of the Poor for the term of 50 years
1832

First Stone laid
  R Caplen
  S Pring   Churchwardens

The Island took the Reform Bill of 1832 in a big way. It needed to, because the effect of the new Act was to reduce the number of Island MPs from six to two – one for the borough of Newport and one for the county of the Isle of Wight. The local radicals at least celebrated the extension of the franchise (less MPs, but more people to vote) and on Saturday 18 August there was a big celebratory dinner and procession in Newport. Then on Thursday 6th September, also in Newport, 1300 poor people were given a dinner at a large hall in Quay Street.

Celebrations though had begun ahead of the event. The *Hampshire Advertiser and Salisbury Guardian* reported the laying, on 6 January, of the foundation stone of a new quay now under construction at the lower end of Newport High Street. 'We understand it is leased for the benefit of the poor for 50 years.' The main purpose of the wharf was for landing cheap coal for the use of the poor; in due course the coal came, but the Overseers had a nail-biting time deciding who were the deserving cases to receive it. When in the 1970s a river improvement scheme began, the commemorative stones were transferred to their present home in the bridge wall.

29 Some Rather Old Timber

Position. Off Hanover Point near Brook
Map Ref. SZ 3790/8370

Note. On a rock shelf off Hanover Point – between Brook Bay and
Compton Bay – at low tide you can see a cluster of petrified tree tunks,
a famous geological feature known as the Pine Raft. They are thought
to be relics of a wide river valley in the Cretaceous period – the age of
the dinosaurs, some 120 million years ago – and we are looking not at a
piece of ancient woodland but at a fossilized log-jam, for these tree
trunks were carried into their present position by the flood waters of a
river (the English Channel as we now know it had yet to be invented!).

Some of the tree tunks have been identified as a primitive form of a
tree not unlike our Monkey Puzzle, *Araucaria imbricatar*, and on their
rather spiky foliage dinosaurs such as the iguanodon would have fed.

Why is it called the Pine Raft? The name was introduced by a 19th-
century geologist, G. A. Mantell. Describing these fossilized trees in
his *Geological Excursions round the Isle of Wight* (1847) he wrote: 'This
accumulation of fossil trees resembles the rafts, as they are termed,
that are annually brought down from the interior of the country by the
tributary streams of the great rivers of North America, and which,
hurried along by those vast floods, entangle in their course the remains
of animals and plants that may happen to lie in the beds of the rivers, or
be floating in the waters'.

A fossilized tree exposed at low tide in the Pine Raft off Hanover Point.

64

30 A Cold Tale from Totland

Position. Moons Hill, Totland
Map Ref. SZ3290/8601

Note. On the north side of the minor road from Farringford to Moons Hill and Alum Bay, one mile east of the junction with B3322, are two domed stone structures with pygmy Romanesque entrances, rather like petrified igloos. They are in fact the opposite of igloos, being designed to keep the cold in rather than out. They are ice houses.

The use of snow and ice for domestic purposes was known in antiquity, but the construction of these thermal shelters for storage of winter gleanings of ice reached England in the later 1600s, and by the 18th century many stately homes had an ice house somewhere in the grounds. The emphasis was on gathering and storing rather than on making ice, though the immersion of vessels in a saltpetre solution to induce chilling had been known and practised since the 16th century.

The ice house, like the later Aga cooker, depended on efficient lagging: thick stone walls, usually lined internally with brick, and final straw packing for the ice and snow. The use of the ice house was much the same as that of a modern fridge/freezer except that you had to trot across your park instead of stroll across the kitchen. The ice was used for chilling drinks, for cooling rooms, or for abating fevers; and food needing chilled storage could be kept in the ice house.

The discovery of these Totland ice houses, during road widening in the late 19th century, caused quite a flutter, and Robert Walker a local antiquary produced a booklet *Phoenicia in Freshwater* speculating on the prehistoric origins of the buildings. Several examples of ice houses are now known in the Island. These at Totland were probably attached to Weston Manor; and, like their fellows, did not a ha'p'orth of harm to the ozone layer!

31 The Submarine that Vanished

Position. Maritime Museum, Sherbourne Street, Bembridge
Map Ref. SZ 6449/8835

Note. On 7 November 1940 the 'S' class submarine HMS Swordfish set
out from Portsmouth for a patrol in the Bay of Biscay. Nothing more
was heard from it. The sub had vanished, and it was finally assumed
that it had been sunk by a German destroyer in its patrol area off Brest.
Its disappearance however remained something of a mystery.

It was in June 1983 that a local diver Martin Woodward found and
identified the wreck of HMS Swordfish just to the south of St
Catherine's Point, the southerly tip of the Isle of Wight. Early in its
voyage the sub had hit a mine.

The story of this remarkable piece of detection is set out in the
Maritime Museum at Bembridge. As well as copies of press accounts
there are items recovered from Swordfish – a brass hatch wheel, and
the conning tower ladder rungs – and a vivid sonar picture of the
wrecked submarine lying on the sea bed at a depth of 150 feet. The
general reaction of surviving relatives of the crew had been relief at
least to know what had happened.

The other parts of the museum collection show how dangerous the
Island coast can be, especially in the days of sailing ships, even without
the added hazards of war. There are relics from offshore wrecks over
hundreds of years.

H.M.S. Swordfish *before its loss in 1940.*

A sidescan sonar trace of the Swordfish.

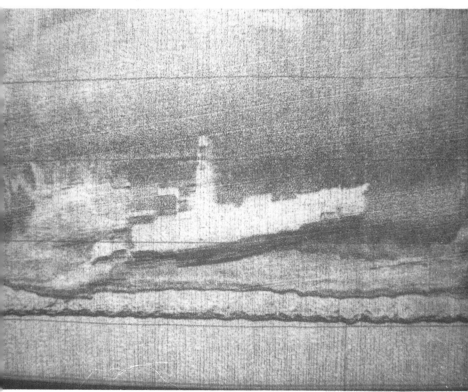

32 The Town Hall without a Town

Position. Newtown
Map Ref. SZ4239/9057

Note. Newtown town hall stands bravely on its green field site, strong on scenery and weak in population. It was an ancient town, a medieval plantation that never really took off. Its economic base, such as it was, was at least diverse: farming, fishing, saltpans, and woodland husbandry. Its faltering growth took a hard knock from a French incursion in 1377, and it seems always to have had more fields than buildings. An account of the town in 1559 said that 'ther is now nother market nor almost no good howse standyng'. Yet in the Parliament of 1584 the town was granted two MPs, and it kept this representation until the Reform Act of 1832, a classic rotten borough. For much of the town's history two families between them controlled all the burgage tenements (the properties carrying votes) and each family nominated one MP and took turns to nominate the Mayor. On the eve of the Reform Act, Parliamentary elections took the form of an oyster dinner in the town hall, at which the chairman would produce a slip of paper carrying the names of the two chosen members, in whose honour a toast would be drunk.

The present town hall was built in the 1690s, though it seems to incorporate traces of an earlier building. It is now owned by the National Trust.

The smuggler's gravestone, Binstead.

33 A Smuggler's Gravestone

Position. Churchyard of the Holy Cross, Binstead
Map Ref: SZ5754/9280

Note. One of the gravestones in Binstead churchyard has at the top a
lively relief carving of an 18th-century sloop in full sail; but the tale that
follows is sad indeed:

To the Memory of Thos Sivell
who was cruely shot on board his
sloop by some officers of the customs
of the Port of Portsmouth on the
15th of June 1785 at the age of 64 years
leaving a disconsolate Widow & family

and it goes on:

All you that pass pray look and see
How soon my life was took from me
By those officers as you hear
They spill'd my Blood that was so dear
But GOD is Good is Just and true
And will reward to each their due

This year was indeed rather a lean time for the many smugglers in
Solent waters because the revenue officers had assembled a formidable
flotilla of fast vessels. Two cutters operating from Cowes covered sixty
miles of coast from Lyme Regis to Beachy Head, backed up by four
cutters under the customs flag (two of them based on Portsmouth, one
on Southampton, one at Chichester), and by two vessels from the
Royal Navy. So, poor Thomas Sivell had the cards stacked against him.

His gravestone is near the south-east corner of the church and is most
easily approached by the second gateway a few yards east of the main
churchyard gate.

34 The Well Worked by a Donkey

Position. Carisbrooke Castle
Map Ref. SZ4861/8777

Note. The feature that distinguishes Carisbrooke from other medieval
castles is its donkey-powered well wheel which, until the 19th century,
kept the castle supplied with fresh spring water, and which is still kept
going today – by a not very hard-worked rota of donkeys duly trained
for the operation – so that visitors may see the great winding wheel in
action.

Donkeys have done this work for time out of memory. The well itself
dates to the 12th century, and the castle accounts of the 13th century
mention the well wheel; but the earliest traceable reference to a
donkey is by Celia Fiennes in about 1696: 'There is a deep well of 40
fathom, they draw up the bucket by a great Wheele in which they put a
horse or ass, a stone thrown down sounds a long tyme ere you hear it
splash into the water'. The donkey wheel was a show piece long before
the age of tourism, and 18th century visitors who enjoyed seeing it in
action included the evangelist John Wesley and the composer Joseph
Haydn.

The well, in the middle of the courtyard, is in a stone well-house of
the 1580s, and the framework of the winding wheel is of the same
period (though the treads and the spindle are modern). The original
castle well seems to have been the one up in the high keep tower, and
this disgraced itself by drying up during the first siege (in 1136 in the
civil wars of Stephen and Matilda). The donkey well though is a show
that still runs, and it even featured in fiction – John Meade Falkner's
smuggling tale *Moonfleet* (1898).

35 A Hilltop Monument to an Egyptian Battle

Position. Havenstreet
Map Ref. SZ5646/9080

Note. If, from the north end of Havenstreet's main street, you look
farther north towards the corner of Firestone Copse, you will see on
the skyline, in the middle of an adjoining field, an intriguing walled
enclosure containing a stone building with an openwork iron cross at
each end of the roof ridge.

Inside the open-fronted building is a shrine in memory of 2nd
Lieutenant Richard Thomas Cyril Willis-Fleming, killed in action at
the battle of Romani in the First World War. This was a field much
more distant than Flanders. In the early months of 1916 a British force
under General Sir Archibald Murray had been engaged on extending
eastwards into the Sinai Desert the Suez Canal defences. On 4 August,
the second anniversary of Britain's declaration of war on Germany, the
British army encountered a strong Turkish/German force at Romani
near the Mediterranean coast of Sinai, and after a heavy battle they
opened the way for an advance to El Arish, and later to Gaza. Young
Willis-Fleming was just twenty – his birthday was the day before the
battle – and his parents who lived at Binstead House put up this shrine
in his memory. It also serves as a memorial for those others from the
parishes of Binstead and Havenstreet who gave their lives in the 1914-
19 war. So it continues to link the rich cattle pasture of Havenstreet
with the sands of Sinai.

36 The Stone that gave a Name to a Village

Position. Mottistone
Map Ref. SZ4063/8421
Access. Footpath off the B3399 immediately west of Mottistone Manor

Note. The charming village of Mottistone takes its name from an ancient monument on the downland to the north, a site called the Long Stone. Actually there are two stones – hefty pieces not native to the local geology – one standing and the other lying on the ground.

The Old English derivation of Mottistone means 'the stone of the speakers' suggesting that in Saxon times this was a place of assembly particularly where legal causes were pleaded: the 'moot halls' that are sometimes found elsewhere reflect the same idea.

The Long Stone, though, goes much farther back into prehistory. To the west of the two stones is the low mound of a long barrow of the kind associated with the burials of the earliest farmers in Britain, from about 3000 BC onwards. Long barrows are uncommon in the Island – surviving traces are known of only three – but the unique feature of this one is the stone setting, more in the megalithic or 'big stone' tradition of the prehistoric tombs of the highland region in the west and north of Britain. The two stones may be the partial remains of a burial chamber, or simply ritual markers at the wide end of the mound; and the mound itself, though hardly discernible, was confirmed by excavation in the 1950s which uncovered its outer ditch and fragments of neolithic pottery.

The Long Stone, always picturesque, is specially worth a visit at bluebell time.

37 A Medieval Lighthouse

Position. St Catherine's Down
Map Ref. SZ 4938/7729
Access. Steep climb by footpath opposite Viewpoint Car Park on the
A3055 just east of Blackgang (Map Ref. SZ4910/7880), signposted
St Catherine's Oratory.

Note. The only surviving medieval lighthouse in Britain is the rocket-
like structure, locally known as the Pepper Pot, on Chale Down. The
date of its building is not known, but it was there in 1312. There was a
small chantry chapel on the east side of the lighthouse tower, but after
the suppression of the chantries in 1547 the deserted building became a
quarry for stone-robbers, and by 1575 the chapel ruins were being used
as a shepherd's shelter. Today nothing of the chapel shows above
ground but the tower remains as an impressive monument to its
medieval builders.

   Its helpfulness to shipping would have been impaired by the fact that
its hilltop site is often shrouded in mist. Indeed a notorious shipwreck
happened on the coast below it on 22 April 1313 when the *Ship of
Blessed Mary* carrying 174 barrels of white wine loaded at Tonnay in
Aquitaine was driven aground, and much of the cargo – in best *Whisky
Galore* style – disappeared down the throats of thirsty islanders. This
was followed by prolonged litigation by the owners and, according to
local folklore, the lighthouse was built by one of the culprits as a
penance. The surviving documents however hardly fit this tradition.

38 The Plague Gateway

Position. Church Litten, Newport
Map Ref. SZ5001/8898

Note. Church Litten park in Newport has no surviving original wall or fence, but in its modern boundary is a splendid Elizabethan gateway, a handsome stone arch built at a stressful time in the town's history.

Late in 1582 Newport was hit by the bubonic plague. The outbreak lasted for eighteen months, and 206 people died, out of a town population of some 1300 or 1400.

At this time Newport had a church but no burial ground, being still part of the parish of Carisbrooke a mile to the west. With the surge of plague burials the Bishop of Winchester gave a licence for the town to have its own cemetery on a site then known as Cosham, and on the Sunday after the licence arrived all the townspeople had to assemble there to work on the enclosure of the area against animals. So began Church Litten ('litten' comes from a Saxon word meaning a cemetery), and the area has been an open space since the 1950s.

During the plague a weekly tax was levied on those who could pay, ranging from four pence for the richer merchants, down to a halfpenny for shoemakers and fishmongers. The money was put to two main uses: paying for the burial of poor people (average cost, four pence), and funding the supposed remedial policy of house quarantine with consequent loss of livelihood for those kept in. The plague accounts contain entries like: 'Mony to sopport them that was willed to kepe the howsse that the syckenes wasse in' and 'payd unto them that wase willed to kepe in for the savyng of the plage'.

39 Ghost of a Fort

Position. Sandown: western corner of Sandham Grounds
Map Ref. SZ6044/8471
Access. From car park in Fort Street.

Note. Sandown Bay with its gently shelving beach has always been a welcoming way in for invaders. The first person to make any attempt at fortification was Henry VIII who towards the end of his reign, in the 1540s, built a square fort at the north-eastern end of the bay.

It wasn't very well placed. In less than a century the sea gratefully ate

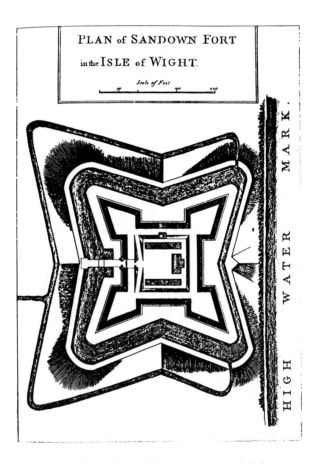

Plan of Sandown Fort. The feeder ditch for the moat is on the left.

it up, and it fell to Charles I to order the remaining ruins to be carted away, and a new fort to be built farther to the north-east. This was of square design with an arrowhead bastion at each corner, and an enclosing moat. It was begun in 1632 and completed in 1636; and proved to be of no use at all to Charles I because – when the Civil War began in 1642 – the small garrison fell over themselves to surrender the fort to Parliament.

It mouldered on over succceeding centuries, finally to be demolished late in the 19th century and replaced in its turn by a third fort – the granite fort, now housing the zoo – to the north-east. The site of Charles I's fort is now underneath the tennis courts of Sandham Grounds; but its 'ghost' can still be seen. The enclosing moat had followed roughly the square of the fort perimeter with each side dented in to a flattened V, thus allowing for the projecting corner bastions. The moat in turn was supplied with water from a spring in the marsh to the north, through a feeder ditch which followed the flattened V outline of the northern piece of moat; and this ditch is still there, the only remaining witness to Charles I's fort building.

The ditch as it is today.

40 The Island's only Medieval Pulpit

Position. St Peter's Church, Shorwell
Map Ref. SZ4574/8300

Note. The Isle of Wight is well provided with medieval churches, but
only one – St Peter's, Shorwell – has a pulpit of that period; and there is
a reason for this.

Medieval parish worship in the Island generally followed the Sarum
rite – a framework of services created for Salisbury Cathedral –
comprising litanies, recitation of psalms, and above all the Mass; so the
altar was the central point in a church. In the 14th century John
Wycliffe complained that the Sarum service 'did hinder the Gospel'
and the recitation of the offices made 'men weary and indisposed to
study God's Law for aching heads'.

Such preaching as the ordinary parish clergy undertook was
generally delivered from the chancel step; but in the 13th century
preaching orders like the Franciscans and the Dominicans began to
bring out the importance of the sermon, and Shorwell church – dating
from about this time – has a fine stone pulpit as part of its north arcade.
Features like this remained exceptional, and not until the Reformation
period did Edward VI order, in 1547, that each parish church should
provide 'a comely and honest pulpit'. In 1620 the Shorwell pulpit was
improved with a wooden tester or sounding board.

On the north wall of this interesting church is a 15th-century wall-
painting of the legend of St Christopher.

41 The Elizabethans at Play: The Brading Bull Ring

Position. Brading
Map Ref. SZ6059/8705

Note. Anchored in a pedestrian crossing island at the south end of Brading High Street is a heavy steel ring: the famous bull ring.

It is the only visible survival on the Island of the former cruel practice of bull-baiting in which the animal, tethered to a ring like this, would be goaded by mastiffs before being slaughtered.

This custom went on for several centuries, being finally outlawed by Parliament in 1835, but it was particularly common in the 16th century.

There were two reasons for it. Firstly the baiting provided a public entertainment in an age that was in many ways perhaps less compassionate than ours, though not without its defenders of animal rights. Philip Stubbes in his *Anatomie of Abuses* (1583) wrote : 'What Christian heart can take pleasure to see one poor beast to rend, tear and kill another, and all for his foolish pleasure?'

There was however a more practical reason for bull-baiting: the belief that it actually improved the quality of the meat when the bull was slaughtered. Woe betide a butcher who sold unbaited meat; like William Waldron, a Brading butcher who at Christmas 1593 'did by a bull of Mr Fuller and him killed befoer Daie at the shopp of William Stilman'. For this, according to the town records, Waldron was fined the going rate for such an offence, 6s 8d – rather more than the average week's wage of a labourer at that time.

42 The Gate to Nowhere

Position. Knighton
Map Ref. SZ 5659/8716

Note. On the eastern verge of Knighton Shute, just by the Footpath
NC4 fingerpost as you come down the hill after turning south from the
Ashey/Downend road (signposted Knighton, Newchurch) is a farm
gate hung from stone gateposts that were clearly intended for higher
things.

   This is the entrance to, and all that is left of, Knighton Gorges, a
large Elizabethan manor house which – in the 18th century at least –
also sported an ornamental lake. This domestic splendour ceased to
exist, in strange circumstances, in 1821.

   The owner at the time was George Bisset, a distant descendant of the

The entrance to Knighton Gorges.

Dillingtons who had rebuilt the house in all its grandeur in the 16th
century. Bisset, an officer in the Hampshire Militia, made Knighton
Gorges a centre of artistic society, his guests including Sir Joshua
Reynolds and David Garrick. An end to this sociability came with a
notorious court case in 1782 when a neighbouring landowner Sir
Richard Worsley of Appuldurcombe sued Bisset for £20,000 damages
for eloping with Worsley's wife Dorothy. (The court found for Worsley
but awarded him only a shilling damages.) Bisset now lived quietly at
Knighton, married, and had two daughters.

It was the elder daughter's matrimonial plans that sounded the death
knell of the house. She planned to marry her clergyman cousin, at
which George Bisset demurred and added that if the couple married
they would never set foot in the house again. They did marry, and they
never did set foot in the house again. In 1821, in his dying months,
Bisset moved into one of the estate cottages and ordered the complete
demolition of Knighton Gorges. That is why we now have at the
roadside of the Shute a gate that leads to nowhere.

Knighton Gorges before its demolition in 1821.

43 An Experiment with Time

Position. Bembridge
Map Ref. SZ6448/8832

Note. It stands like Dr Who's Tardis in Bembridge High Street facing
down Sherbourne Street. Looking at this telephone kiosk we think we
are in the 1920s; but inside is the latest British Telecom push-button
equipment: a happy blend of history and modern technology.

The first outside telephone kiosks in Britain were put up by the
National Telephone Company in 1908. They justified the name of
kiosk, for there was no standard pattern and some of them were shady
arbours designed to blend with parkland settings. Very soon
afterwards the Post Office started installing their own kiosks, many
with a coin-operated door, so that the caller paid at an early stage in the
operation. Most of these phone boxes were wooden, but in the tougher
areas some were made of galvanized iron to resist attempts to kick the
door down if the coin mechanism failed to work.

The first standardized design, by the Post Office Engineering

Department, was in 1921 with the model K.1 (Kiosk No. 1). It was a prefabricated box in reinforced concrete, with a red wooden door and metal glazing bars. The first models cost about £35 to make, but production runs brought the cost down to £15. The Bembridge box, elegantly crowned with metal work topped with a spear-shaped finial, is one of these K.1 boxes. It was installed on 28 August 1929, when Ramsay MacDonald was Prime Minister; and, according to British Telecom, it is the only one of its kind in the Southern Region. It is now owned and maintained by South Wight Borough Council, while the telephone inside it is part of the normal British Telecom system.

Yarmouth tide mill.

44 The Mill Sabotaged by a Railway

Position. Yarmouth
Map Ref. SZ3565/8932
Access. By Station Road on to the Public Bridleway Y19 to Freshwater
(the old railway track) which passes south of the building. The mill is
now a private house.

Note. The fine Georgian building of Yarmouth Mill is now a private
dwelling, and none of its machinery survives, but it is interesting as
being the only visible relic of the Island's tide mills; another at Wootton
Bridge, with its machinery, was demolished as recently as the 1960s.

Where the Thorley Brook flows into the Yar estuary from the east a
mill dam was built, with the tide mill at the Yarmouth end of it. The
three northern bays of the building housed the mill, and the miller's
house was in the southern three.

The mill was built in 1793 and this date reflects the urgent need for
grain processing at that time. The beginning of war with France meant
that farm prices were buoyant in face of the continuing demands for
flour supplies for the army and navy. Hitherto uneconomic marginal
land was brought under cultivation, and at this period the Isle of Wight
was producing seven times its own consumption of grain. New, big
flour mills were needed, and Yarmouth Mill was part of the answer. It
was a case of demand generating supply.

A later upheaval, the building of the Freshwater to Newport Railway
in the 1880s, is thought by some industrial historians to have
contributed to the final demise of the mill. Its mill pond was crossed by
the viaduct and embankment of the new railway about a hundred yards
from the mill; and if, as seems likely, this reduced the water flow in the
tidal pond, loss of power could have meant loss of earnings – and there
is evidence that an auxiliary steam engine was put in. One hopes that
the railway company, as its trains chuffed past the decaying mill, spared
an occasional load of cheap coal for the mill engine.

45 The Elephant that Founded a Hospital

Position. Adelaide Grove, East Cowes
Map Ref. SZ5050/9538

Note. The Frank James Hospital at East Cowes has an unusual history.
Frank Linsley James was the eldest son of a wealthy Liverpool metal
merchant. After graduating at Cambridge he took to pursuing an early
interest in travel – and it was travel on the grand scale. In the winter of
1877-8 he went into the Sudan as far as Berber, travelling by the Nile
and through the Korosko Desert, finally returning across the desert to
Dongola. The following winter he joined a military expedition led by
Sir Samuel Browne (he of the Sam Browne belt) up the Khyber Pass to
Jellalabad. There followed two more seasons of further exploration in
and around the Sudan. Then in 1882-3 he began to apply his attention
to Mexico. 1884 saw the start of an extended expedition into the Horn
of Africa, reaching areas to which Burton and Speke had never
managed to penetrate. His remarkable achievement of taking a
caravan of nearly a hundred people and as many camels on a thirteen-
day journey across a waterless waste in the course of getting as far south
as the Webbe Shebeyli River led Lord Aberdare – in his annual address
to the Royal Geographical Society the following year – to describe
James's expedition as one of the most interesting and difficult in all
recent African travel. James returned to England with a collection of
flora which he presented to the Kew Herbarium, and one of
lepidoptera which he gave to the natural history branch of the British
Museum. He then had a short quiet interval writing a book, *The
Unknown Horn of Africa* (1888).

Very soon he was at his exploring again. A member of the Royal
Yacht Squadron, he set off in his yacht *The Lancashire Witch* to visit
such varied places as the Persian Gulf, Spitzbergen, and Novaya
Zemlya. Then, early in 1890 he set out on what was to prove his last
venture, a series of explorations inland from the West African coast.
On 21 April 1890, with *The Lancashire Witch* anchored off San Benito
about a hundred miles north of the Gaboon River, he and his
companions landed to explore in from the coast. No more than a mile
from the sea Frank James was killed by an elephant which he and his
party had wounded; and so ended a more than usually eventful life.

To commemorate this remarkable career Frank's two brothers, John
Arthur and William Dodge, together with many of his friends, in 1893
founded and built at East Cowes an almshouse for aged and disabled

sailors; but new needs arose. The South African War began to dominate public attention, and in 1900 the old inmates of the alms-house were pensioned and the building was put into use as a convalescent home for invalided soldiers.

With the coming of peace this need in turned passed, and the donors then offered the home for a trial period of two years, with an annual endowment, to the Island Governor H.R.H. Princess Beatrice, for a cottage hospital for Cowes, East Cowes, and part of the parishes of Whippingham and Northwood. This arrangement soon became virtually permanent, and from 1903 until the coming of the National Health Service in 1948 the cottage hospital, governed by trustees, was sustained by voluntary contributions.

And this chain of events was started by that African elephant, back in 1890.

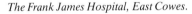

The Frank James Hospital, East Cowes.

46 All Quiet Again on Ashey Down

Position. Ashey Down
Map Ref. SZ5746/8757
Access. Track east from Ashey Road on bend immediately east of the junction with the road to Yarbridge.

Note. The summit of Ashey Down is a good viewpoint, a place where you can see and be seen; and this fact has been gratefully accepted by sailors in their use of the solid, white stump – the Ashey seamark – which was constructed in 1735. Today the top of the down, with its seamark, looks much as it did in the early 1700s.

In the later 1700s though, it was a very different scene, all bustle; and it was all to do with communications. In a variation on the medieval beacon system the Navy built four semaphore stations at key high points in the Island. These relayed to the admiral at Portsmouth details of all shipping seen off the Island; and the final messages all passed through Ashey.

We know, from pictures and descriptions, what Ashey Down was like at the height of its communications boom. The signal station itself was a small, two-roomed building, with an adjoining shed in which the signalling tackle was kept. Near the signal house was set a topmast and a topgallant mast of a man-of-war, with a yard crossing them and set on an east-west axis. The signals were made by raising a certain number of balls at the ends of the yard, and sometimes by hoisting a flag at the end of the topgallant mast. It was all very nautical work, and the station was manned always by a lieutenant, a midshipman, and two seamen. The signal masts were carefully set on the Portsmouth side of the big seamark, to leave clear visibility. Thanks to this system, the commander at Portsmouth had a full picture of all shipping movements within sight of the Island; and even from the most distant station, on the cliffs overlooking the Needles, messages got through to Portsmouth in less than thirty minutes.

It all became part of the passing scene. The 19th century brought the defeat of Napoleon; a long period of peace; and eventually, telegraphy and radio. Now Ashey Down is quiet again, its seamark tranquilly stolid, just as it was before the Navy came bustling in with their semaphores.

John Nixon's late 18th century watercolour showing the seamark and signal station on Ashey Down (see back cover).

The Ashey Down seamark.

47 When Toad Came Home

Position. Rock, north of Brighstone
Map Ref. SZ4240/8428

Note: Readers of Kenneth Grahame's *Wind in the Willows*, seeing a triangular road hazard sign with the legend:

might expect to meet a fast car with a demon driver. Such a sign can indeed be found at Rock on the road from Calbourne to Brighstone, 0.4 miles south of the junction with Strawberry Lane, and it is designed to protect these jolly amphibians as they make their mostly nocturnal crossings of the road. The little valley to the south-west of the road is supplied with water – it even used to run a mill – and at spawning time in about March the toads go hopping down to it, hopping back in about April. The next excitement is in about July when the new generation of young toads, travelling up the hill, first sample for themselves the thrill of crossing the road.

The Island goes in for interesting road signs. Until recently Cedar Hill in Carisbrooke had one reading:

!

D u c k s
in road

for the benefit of a family of mallards, with no traffic sense, that lived in and around the stream at the bottom of Carisbrooke High Street. Still surviving is a sign near the top of Shorwell Shute:

Pedestrians using
carriageway

suggestive more of the Isle of Sark than the Isle of Wight!

48 A Tumulus Cocktail

Position. Brook Down
Map Ref. SZ3900/8520

Note. The Island has an abundance of tumuli or prehistoric burial
mounds, mostly of the Bronze Age. Well over two hundred are
recorded so far; many more must have been ploughed out of sight over
the centuries, but the sites of these 'invisibles' often respond to
continuing aerial survey for crop marks indicating interesting things
under the surface.

   The tops of the downs are the best places to find the surviving
tumulus mounds, because here there is less threat from cultivation.

Brook Down

There have been other threats, of course: digging for treasure is known to have gone on as early as the medieval period, and probably even long before that. Hence we find crater-like depressions in the tops of many mounds. Not that there was really treasure there to rob, though the contents of the burials are interesting for other reasons. The burial itself was usually a cremation inside a rather lumpy, clapped-out pottery urn; but the grave goods accompanying the burial are a reminder of the long reach of European trade about the middle of the second millennium BC when most of these burials took place: occasional gold ornaments and bowls, certainly, but much more bronzework – weapons, tools, and ornaments – and exotic items like amber from the Baltic and lapis lazuli from North Africa.

The interest in looking at the group called the Five Barrows on Brook Down is in the variety of shapes. Excavation has shown that ritual was of prime importance in Bronze Age burials, and even the mound shapes were significant because there are defined types, of which three can be seen at Brook. The common or garden shape was the bowl barrow, like a pudding tipped out of an inverted dish, filling the whole area up to the ditch circle. Then there was the bell barrow which had a smaller mound leaving a flat shelf or berm between it and the ditch. Another type, also at Brook, is the disk barrow with a diminutive mound looking across a wide flat area to the ditch. Sorting out the shapes of the mounds is less easy because of the subsequent efforts the barrow-robbers, but an element of the original variety of design can still be seen in the Five Barrows.

Barrow groups with a number in the name always have an elastic factor. There is a group in Berkshire called the Lambourn Seven Barrows; here an archaeologist claimed to have counted up to thirty mounds before he was chased off the scene by a bull.

49 The Sailors who Waited Nearly 200 Years for Their Memorial

Position. Ryde
Map Ref. SZ5990/9272
Access. Half-way between the Dover Street roundabout and the Canoe Lake, in line with a pedestrian crossing, is a small public garden linking the Esplanade with Monkton Street to the south. The memorial is at the north end of the garden, facing the Esplanade.

Note. Admiral Richard Kempenfelt was a most distinguished and able officer, but his death aboard his flagship the *Royal George* in 1782 is remembered specially because of the general calamity of which it formed part; for about a thousand people were drowned when the vessel went down, and the disaster happened at anchorage in the Solent, within sight of friendly shores.

England was at war. Much of the fleet was heavily engaged in America trying to cope with the seceding colonies there. To increase the Government's problems, France and Spain also declared war, and in the late summer of 1782 Gibraltar was being besieged. On 15 August Lord Howe – under whom Kempenfelt served as a junior admiral – brought his fleet into the Solent with urgent orders to refit before sailing to the relief of Gibraltar. In the course of this work, on 29 August the *Royal George* was given a slight list – by shifting the guns over to one side – in order to expose and repair a badly leaking seam in the hull just below the water line. This put unaccustomed strain on an already rotten hull; the timbers gave way and the ship went down with everyone aboard – some 800 crew and marines, and various visiting tradesmen, wives, and children.

The suddenness of the disaster, and the tragic loss of life, appalled the nation. The public mood was expressed within weeks in Cowper's poem 'Toll for the brave – the brave! that are no more'; and during those same weeks many bodies were washed ashore on the sands around Ryde – at that time just a small fishing village – and had mostly anonymous burials nearby.

They had a long wait for a monument, but this came at last when on 31 August 1965 Earl Mountbatten of Burma – newly installed at Carisbrooke Castle by the Queen, as Governor of the Island – unveiled a memorial plaque in Ashley Gardens, a small, flower-bedded area linking Ryde Esplanade with the bottom of Monkton Street.

The plaque shows Kempenfelt's impressive but mouldering flagship

modelled in low relief alongside an inscription:

In memory of the many officers and men
of the Royal Navy & Royal Marines
who lost their lives when the ROYAL GEORGE
sank at Spithead on the 29th August 1782
and who lie buried along this seafront.
And here by friends unknown, unmarked,
unwept,
THEY REST.

The various sequels of the accident were that the fleet duly sailed and
relieved Gibraltar; and eventually the wreck of the *Royal George*,
which had gone down near a main shipping channel, were blown up in
the early 1800s. The explosive charges were placed by divers and,
interestingly, detonated by an electrical charge.

50 The Man who Ordered his own Burial

Position. The Oglander chapel in St Mary's Church, Brading
Map Ref. SZ6067/8731

Note. Sir John Oglander (1585-1655) is certainly one of the most
interesting Islanders on record. His family had lived at Nunwell near
Brading since Norman times, and the story of the Oglanders is closely
twined with the history of the Island.

Sir John served in various public offices such as Sheriff of
Hampshire, Deputy Governor of Portsmouth, and Deputy Lieutenant
of the Isle of Wight; but it is his personality, rather than his public
image, that comes through most vividly to our own day. He made
almost a fetish of his account books, and his painstaking record of
every penny spent and lent gives a graphic picture of the life of the
country gentry in the early 1600s. The real joy of his account books,
though, is the incidental spillage on to their margins of his observations
on all aspects of life – a raw version of Montaigne or Bacon. He had an
insatiable curiosity about antiquity, but his appetite for the new was

Sir John Oglander's effigy, Brading.

equally keen: seamen's tales of distant lands, a watch bought on a visit to London (price, £7.10s), and 'sheles and hornes and Chiena disches' that he bought from a ship returning from the Far East in 1633.

He always fussed about his health; and once in 1630 he felt so ill that he decided it was high time to arrange his obsequies. 'Make no funeroll for mee', he wrote in a spare piece of his beloved account book, 'but bury mee at the uper end of my Greategrandfathors Toombe'. He survived to decorate this note with the further comment: 'This was when I wase sicke and like to Die'.

At his death in 1655 though, his wishes were faithfully carried out and his tomb stands in Brading church – in the south aisle where the Oglander chapel is – immediately to the east of his great-grandfather Oliver Oglander. The strange thing about this tomb however is the effigy on it: a carving that Sir John had kept stored at Nunwell for the occasion. It shows him not only in armour – that was a general convention – but in full fig as a medieval crusader knight, with his legs crossed. Sir John the antiquary has had the last word.

The figure cannot of course convey to us the appearance of its subject: if it was ever intended to, he aged while the carving did not. We need not worry: Sir John's ever-present account books come to the rescue.

Wouldest thou feign see me, being dead
so many years since? I will give thee
mine own character. Conceive thou sawest
an aged, somewhat corpulent man, of middle
stature, with a white beard and somewhat
big mustaches, riding in black or some
sad-coloured clothes over the downs to
take the air, morning and evening . . . his
hair grey and his complexion very sanguine.

Sir John lives in his writings rather than his monument.

51 The Uncrowned King

Position. Sandown
Map Ref. SZ5952/8418

Note. King Edward VIII had one of the shorter reigns in British history
– 325 days from his accession on 20 January to his abdication on 10
December 1936, even allowing for the leap year. Short as the reign
was, the business of public administration had to go on, and there was
time enough to design and produce at least a few pillar boxes adjusted
to the new Sovereign. One of these, with its E VIII R monogram, can
be seen on the south-west side of Melville Street, Sandown, a few yards
south of its junction with the Broadway. It is one of a select company:
the only other example on the Island is in Green Lane, Shanklin.

Melville Street, Sandown, pillar box.

52 From Zeppelins to Space Invaders: Strange Story of a Hangar

Position. Shanklin Esplanade
Map Ref. SZ5870/8162

Note. This building is a veteran of the 1914-18 War. It is actually an aircraft hangar, and it began life in Bembridge Harbour as a seaplane base used by the Royal Navy and the United States Navy. Peace-time brought a new phase in its life when it was transported to its present site on Shanklin Esplanade to serve as a theatre during the summer season. Today it is still in the entertainment business – humming, buzzing, and flashing its coloured lights as an amusement arcade.

53 Part of Queen Victoria's Water Taxi

Position. Osborne House park, south of Swiss Cottage and Museum
Map Ref. SZ 5261/9476
Access. During normal opening hours. A minibus runs between Osborne House and Swiss Cottage during the summer season.

Note. When in 1846 Queen Victoria and Prince Albert came to live in their newly-acquired Island home at Osborne – still in the course of reconstruction – they inherited the Islanders' age-old problems of living with the Solent crossing. Their royal yacht the *Fairy* outlived the Prince Consort by two years, being replaced in 1863 with the newly-built yacht *Alberta* which was to serve the Queen for the rest of her life, finally carrying her body from East Cowes to Portsmouth after her death in 1901. Now the *Alberta's* forward deckhouse, beautifully restored with its white paint and polished brass, and looking festive under a canvas awning, has been added to the exhibits at Osborne. It stands, next to the Queen's bathing machine, out in the grounds near the Swiss Cottage and Museum.

A vessel of 370 tons with a length of 160 feet and a beam of 22 feet, she had a shallow enough draught to be able to berth at East Cowes even at low water. In all her years of service she had only one bad mishap, when in August 1875 she collided with and sank the yacht *Mistletoe*, with loss of life, which left *Alberta's* crew rather under a cloud. She had a good, active life however, and stayed in service with the royal family until 1912.

The Alberta's *deckhouse, Osborne House.*

Queen Victoria's bathing machine, Osborne House.

54 The Medieval Abbey and the Modern Abbey

Position. Quarr, between Wootton and Binstead
Map Ref. SZ5659/9272 (medieval ruins);
           SZ5623/9269 (modern abbey)
Access. The church of the modern abbey is open to visitors. Access is
by the abbey drive, north turning off the A3054 (no parking in drive or
on verge; there is parking space near the church entrance). For
pedestrian access to the medieval site (not much structure visible,
mainly the precinct wall) turn east from the abbey drive along Public
Bridleway R3 signposted 'Binstead and Abbey Ruins'.

Note. Quarr takes its name from the limestone quarries there, which
were being exploited as early as Roman times, but which are now
worked out. It was this stone that went into Winchester and Chichester
Cathedrals, but the shortest journey it made was to the adjoining abbey
founded by the Lord of the Island, Baldwin de Redvers, in 1131. The
original community was of the Savignac order but it soon merged with
the Cistercians. Quarr had many endowments – granges, farms, mills,
and town properties – in the Island, and these were suddenly dispersed
when Quarr was dissolved, together with the other smaller
monasteries, in 1537. Much of the stone of the abbey was used in Henry
VIII's new coastal forts, and the abbey church was so completely
dismantled that apparently even its exact site was uncertain by the early
1600s.
    We now come to the curious thing: that monks have come back to
Quarr; Benedictines this time, part of the congregation of Solesmes in
France, who came over to the Isle of Wight, first to Appuldurcombe
and then settling at Quarr. Here, next to the medieval site, they began
building their new house in 1908 to a design by one of the monks, a
talented architect Dom Paul Bellot. The abbey was not of stone this
time – the quarries were long since exhausted – but of Belgian brick, a
medium to which the design has been skilfully adapted, especially in
the wonderfully soaring proportions of the abbey church, built in 1911-
1912.

Quarr Abbey, the medieval remains.

Quarr Abbey.

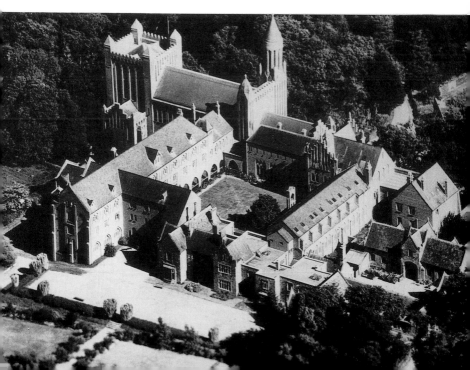

55 The Conspirator who made Good

Position. St Thomas's Church, Newport
Map Ref. SZ4998/8915

Note. In the south aisle of Newport parish church is the tomb of Sir
Edward Horsey, Captain of the Isle of Wight from 1565 until his death
from the plague at Haseley Manor in 1583; and on it is a fine carved
effigy of this buccaneering puritan.

As a young man he became involved in the Dudley conspiracy
against Queen Mary in 1556 but fled abroad quickly enough to escape
arrest. His associates on the Continent were similar rugged puritans –
his tomb inscription describes him as 'fautor evangelii' (maintainer of
the gospel) – and with the accession of Elizabeth in 1558 he returned to
England with all the other protestant exiles. His reward came in 1565
when he was appointed Captain of the Isle of Wight and Vice-Admiral
of Hampshire. The latter post he enjoyed to the full, for he took rather
a flexible view of the boundary between piracy and legitimate
privateering, and got on well with the ruffianly crews of pirates who
made their base at Mead Hole near Wootton. One under-cover agent
investigating these, having had supper with some of Horsey's men one
evening, next day managed to get aboard a pirate ship where stolen
goods were being sold and was startled to find Horsey's men there too.

Sir John Oglander, a local gentlemen of the early 1600s who knew
Horsey only by reputation, described him as 'a brave soldier, but
assuming too much'. Horsey generally seems to have got on well with
the Islanders. He is said to have introduced hares into the Island, and
instead of using the then ruinous Captain's lodgings at Carisbrooke
Castle he lived at Haseley Manor with a Mrs Dowsabell Mills; 'not
without some taxe of incontinencye', wrote Oglander, 'for nothinge
stopped theyr maryadge, but that he had a wyfe alive in Fraunce'.

56 The Arreton Girl who took the Nation by Storm

Position. Arreton churchyard
Map Ref. SZ 5345/8677

Note. Elizabeth Wallbridge did not expect fame, nor did she find it in her lifetime. Born in the late 18th century, the daughter of a farm worker, she lived for a time with her family in their small cottage at Hale Common between Merstone and Sandown. She then went into service at the grandiose Tudor manor house of Knighton Gorges near Newchurch; she wasted away from consumption, and was buried in Arreton churchyard. This may not seem the kind of biography to make

her a national figure, but she was to have a remarkable public relations man – the Reverend Legh Richmond. In 1799, at the age of 27 and fresh from Cambridge, he came to the Island as vicar of Brading and Yaverland. In the years before he left the Isle of Wight in 1805 he was influenced by the writings of William Wilberforce and became swept up in the evangelical revival, himself becoming a preacher of considerable repute, particularly after he became rector of Turvey in Bedfordshire. He had taken away from the Island, however, notes of his experiences in the parishes there, and in 1809 he began to organize his recollections in narrative form. These appeared under a nom de plume in various editions of *The Christian Guardian* between 1809 and 1814. So Elizabeth Wallbridge hit the headlines in the story *The Dairyman's Daughter* which caught the imagination of the whole country, so much so that when – with other Island stories – it came out in book form as *Annals of the Poor* in 1814, Legh Richmond had to rewrite and enlarge it. His book was translated into French, Italian, German, Danish, and Swedish, and it was eagerly read in America. In Richmond's lifetime two million copies were printed in English alone – and it has in our own day had a modern reprint. In 1822 Legh Richmond made a triumphant return to the Island for the erection of memorials to his cottager heroines – Elizabeth Wallbridge at Arreton, little Jane at Brading, the subject of *The Young Cottager*; and *The Negro Servant*, a story set in Sandown. But Elizabeth Wallbridge had started the national enthusiasm.